where's my baby now?

CLAIRE BRETECHER

where's my baby now?

TRANSLATED FROM THE FRENCH
BY ANGELA MASON AND PAT FOGARTY

A Methuen Paperback

First published in France as
le destin de Monique 1983
by the author

First published in Great Britain 1987
by Methuen London Ltd
11 New Fetter Lane, London EC4P 4EE
Copyright © 1983 Claire Bretecher
Translation copyright © 1987 Angela Mason and Pat Fogarty
Printed and bound in Great Britain
by R. J. Acford, Chichester, West Sussex

British Library Cataloguing in Publication Data

Bretecher, Claire
Where's my baby now?
I. Title
741.5′944   PN6747.B/

ISBN 0-413-17120-5

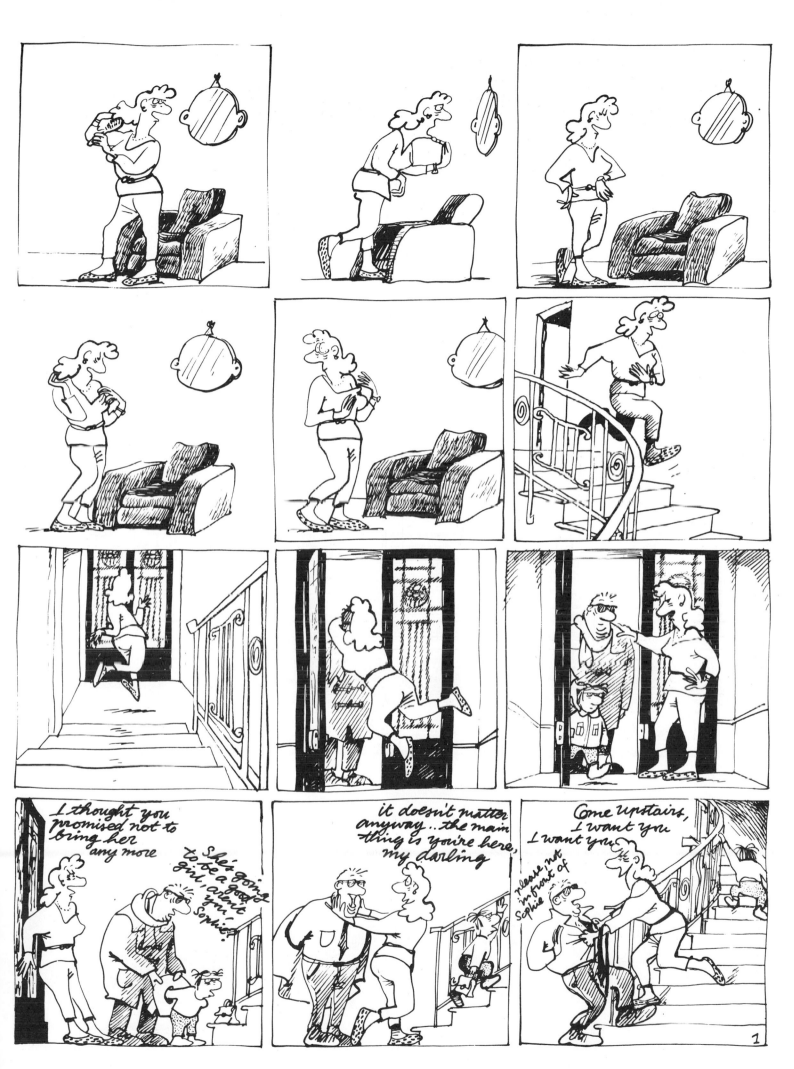

9

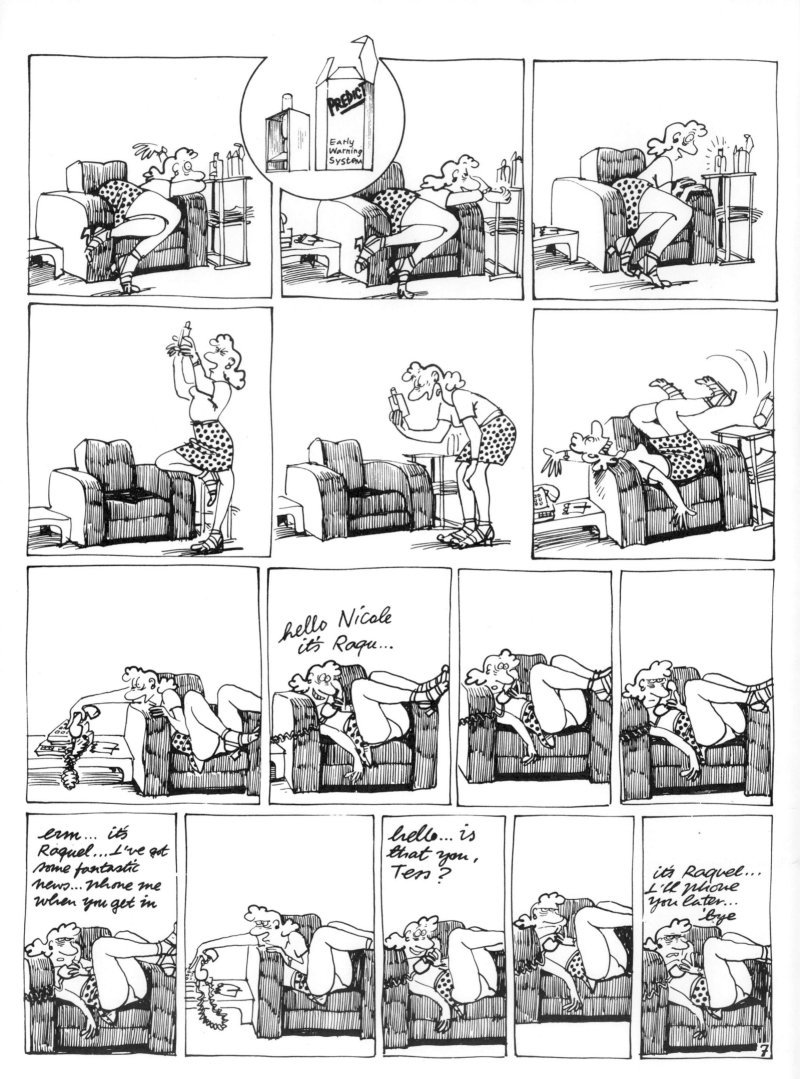

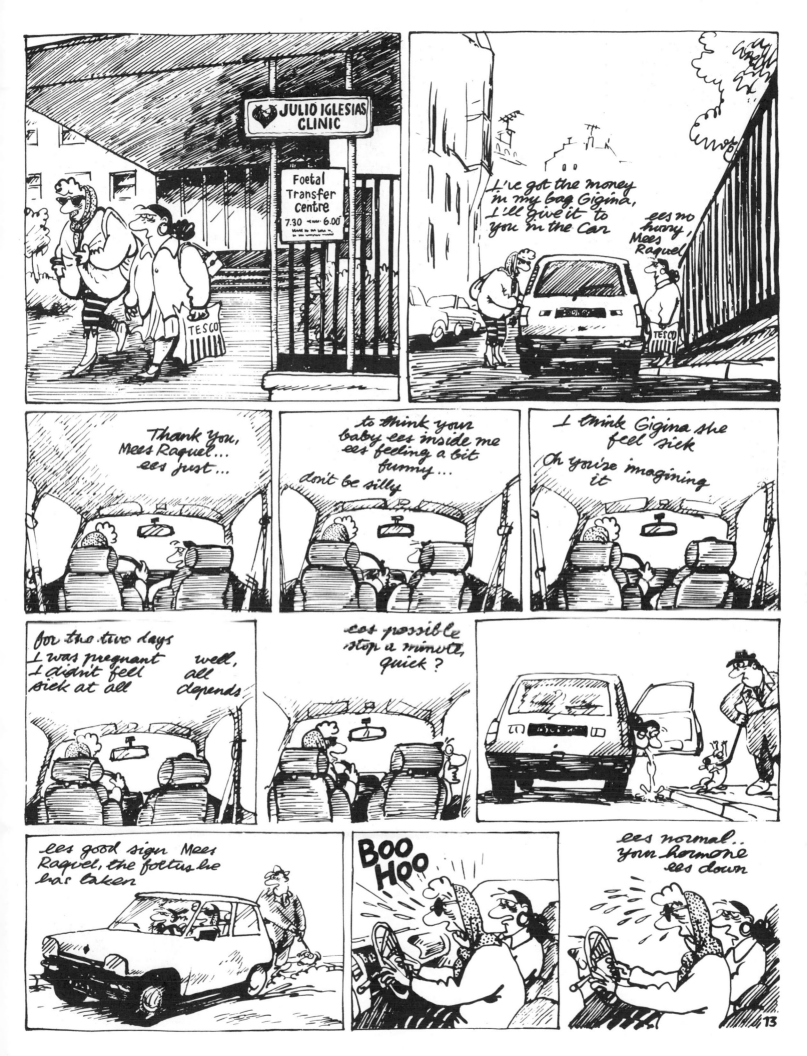

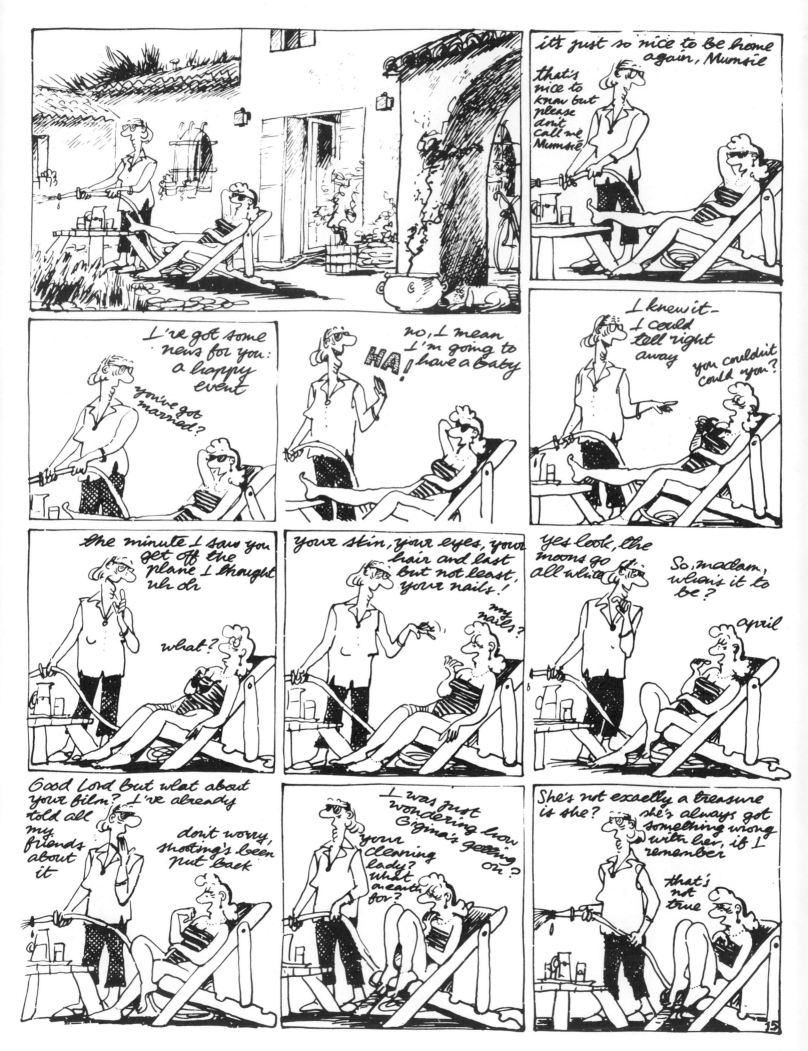

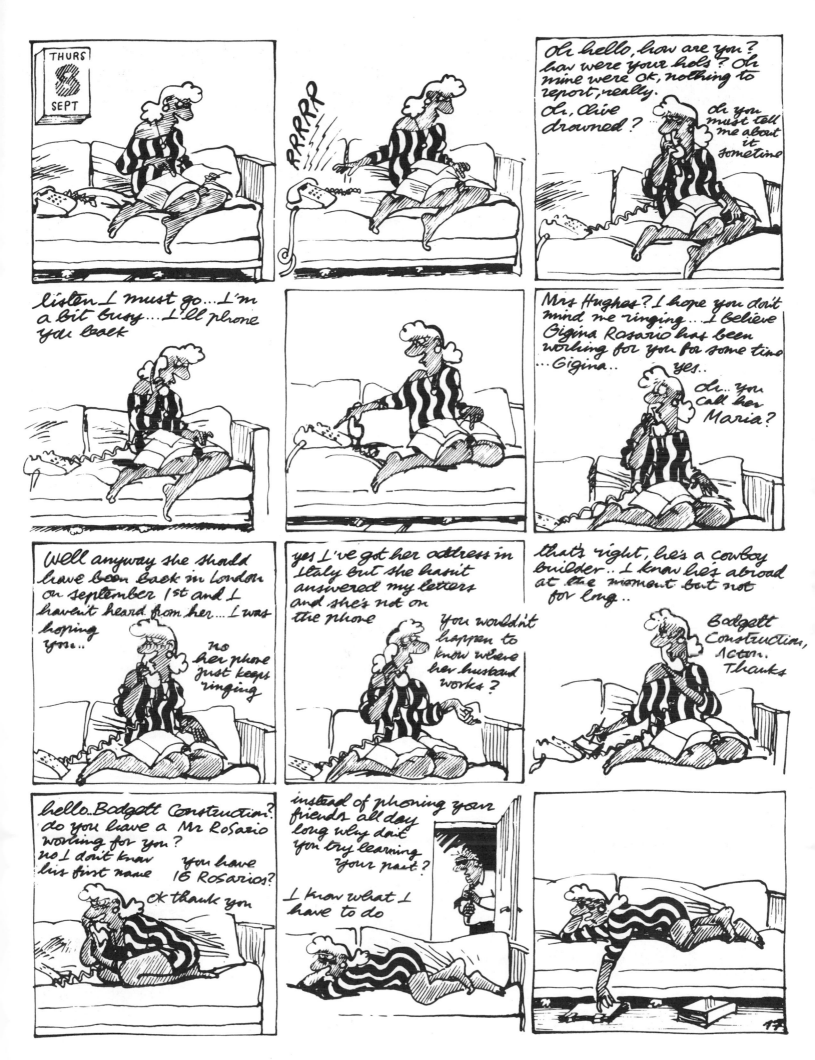

*INDUSTRIAL INJURY BENEFIT

30

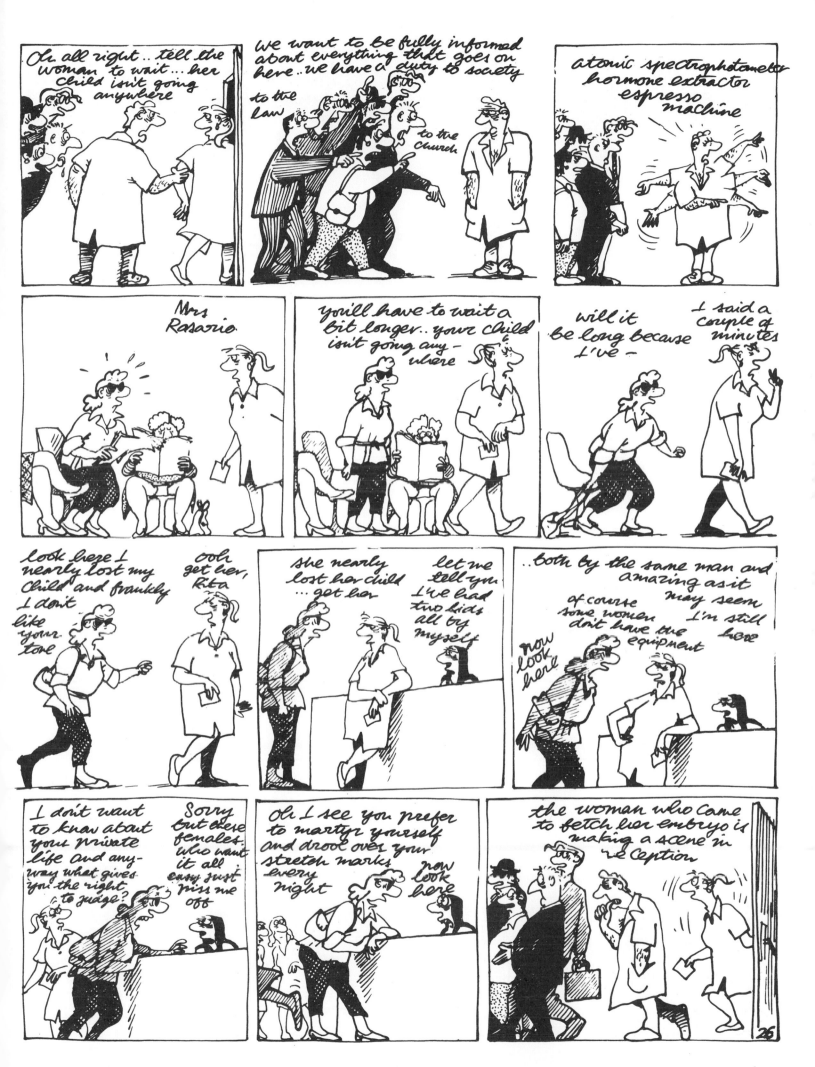

38

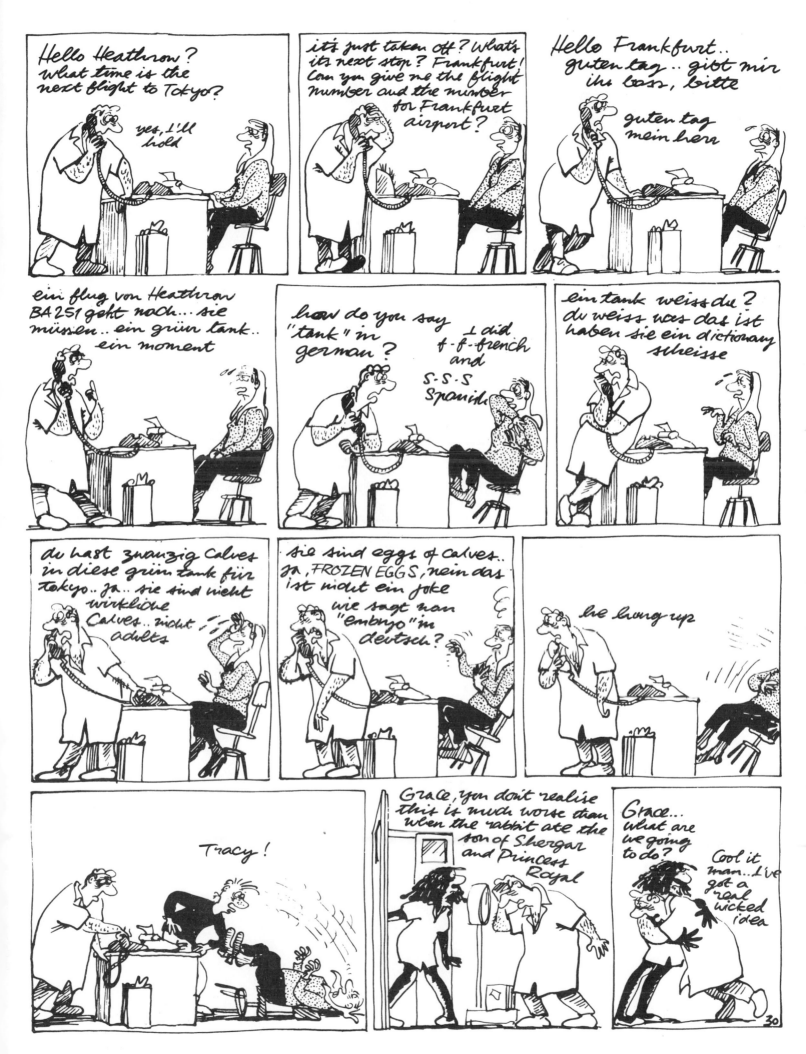

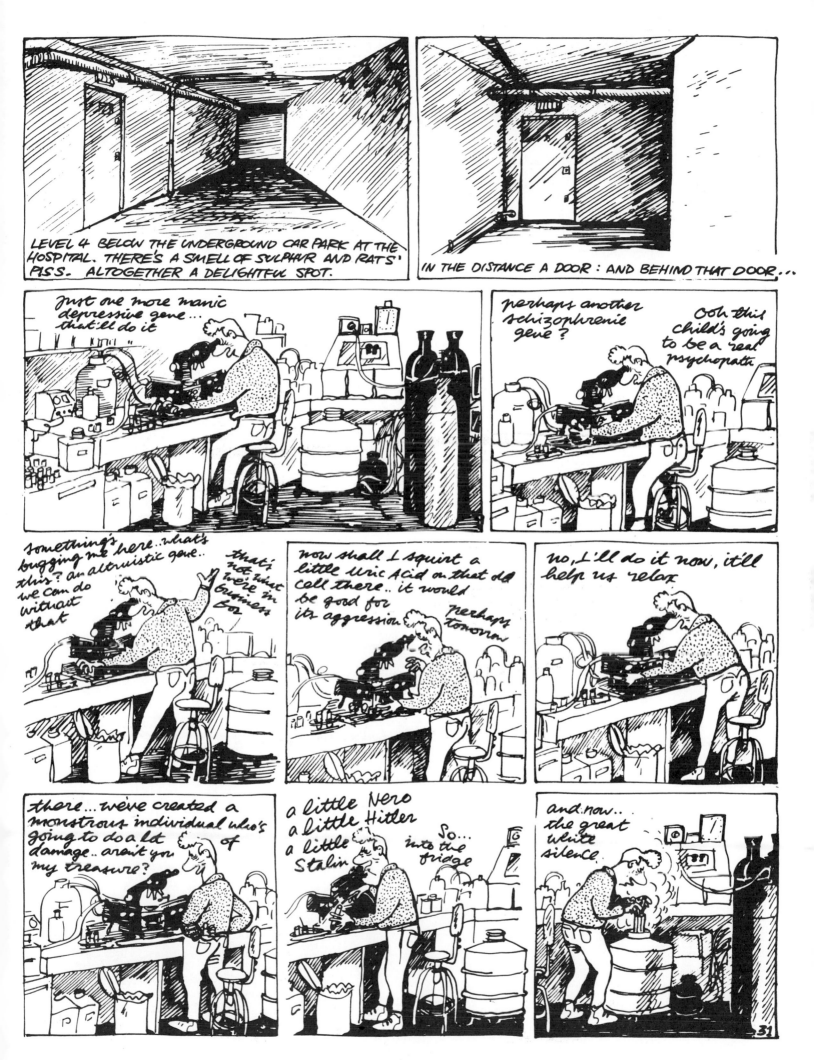

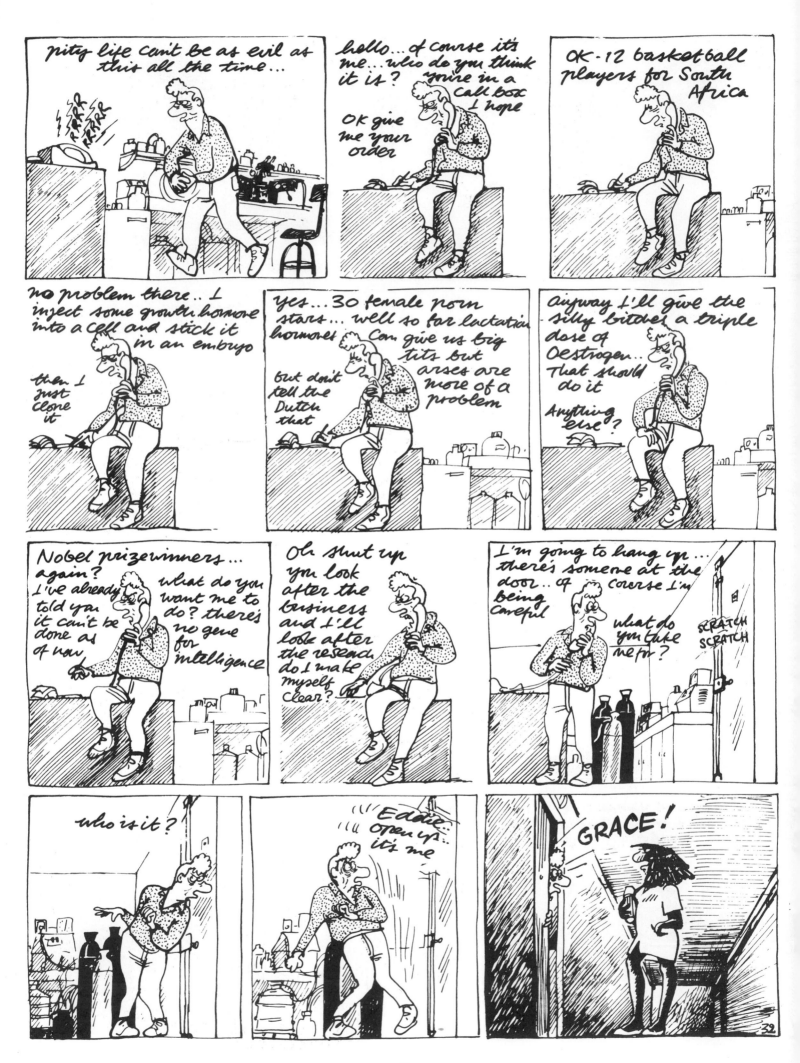

44

46

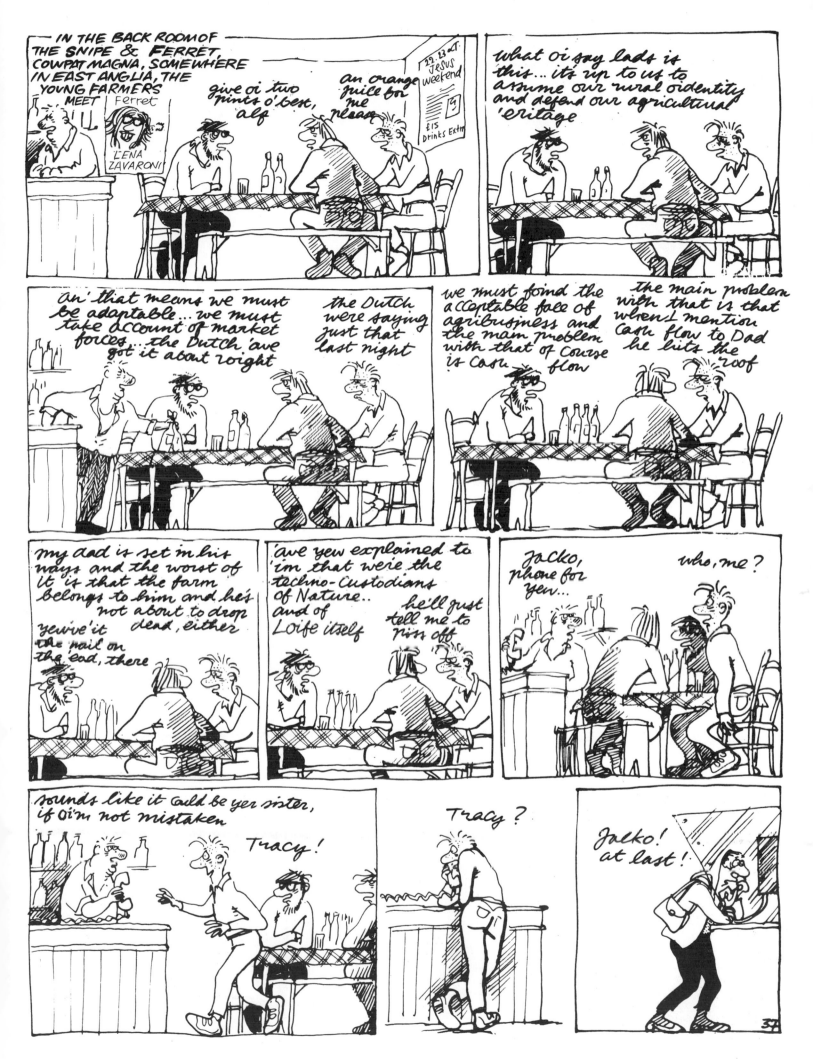

49

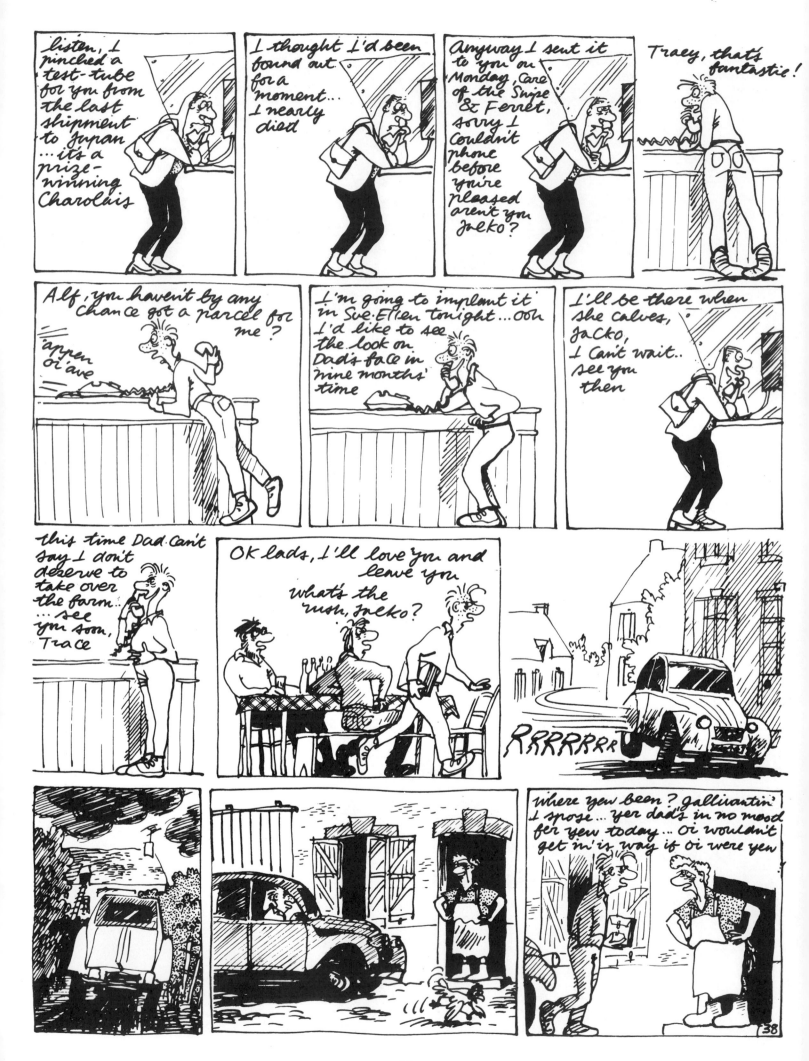

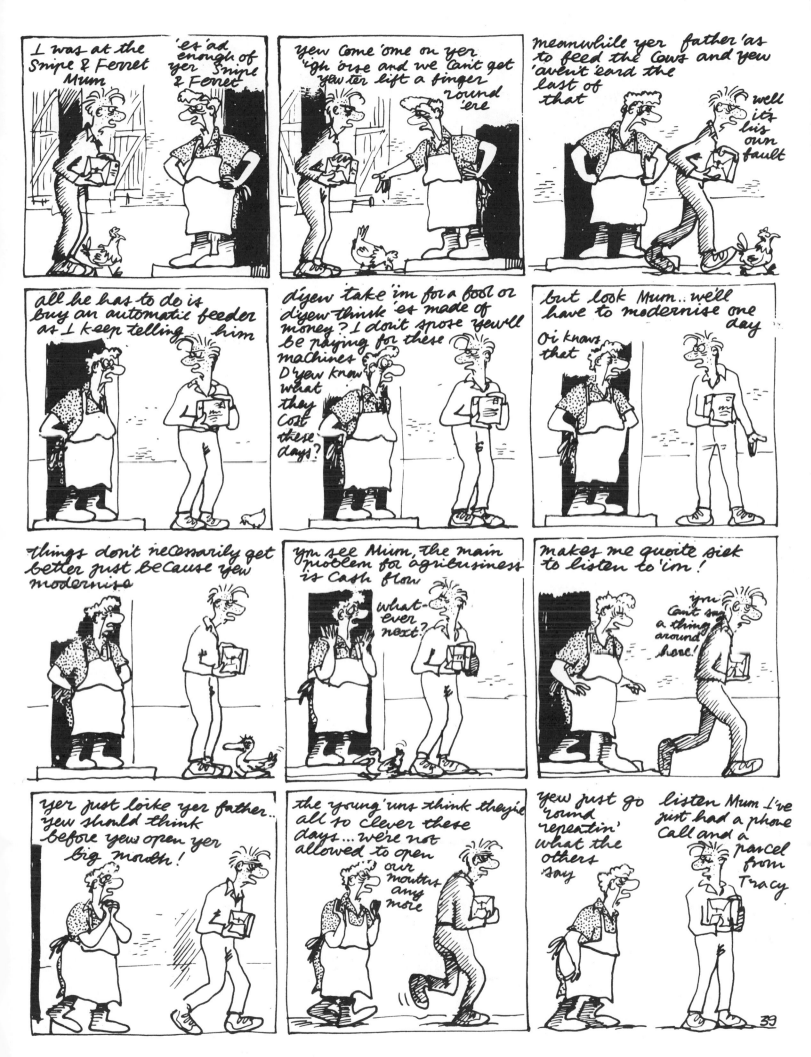

51

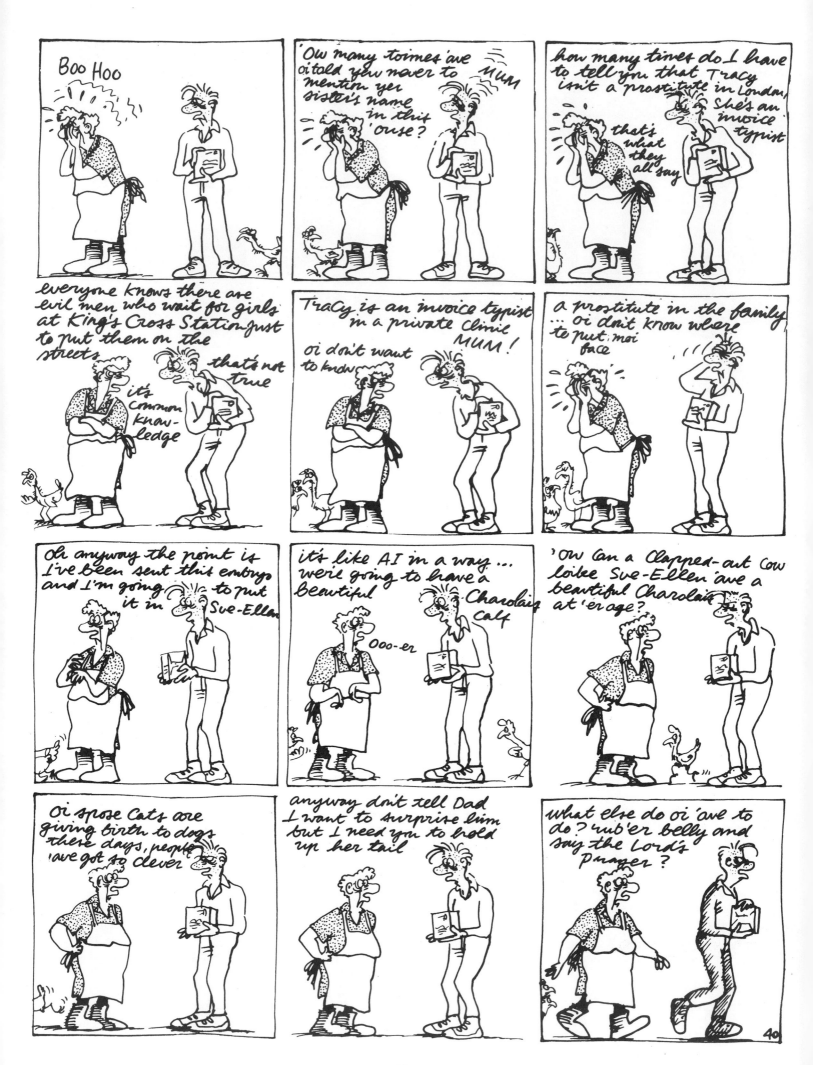

54

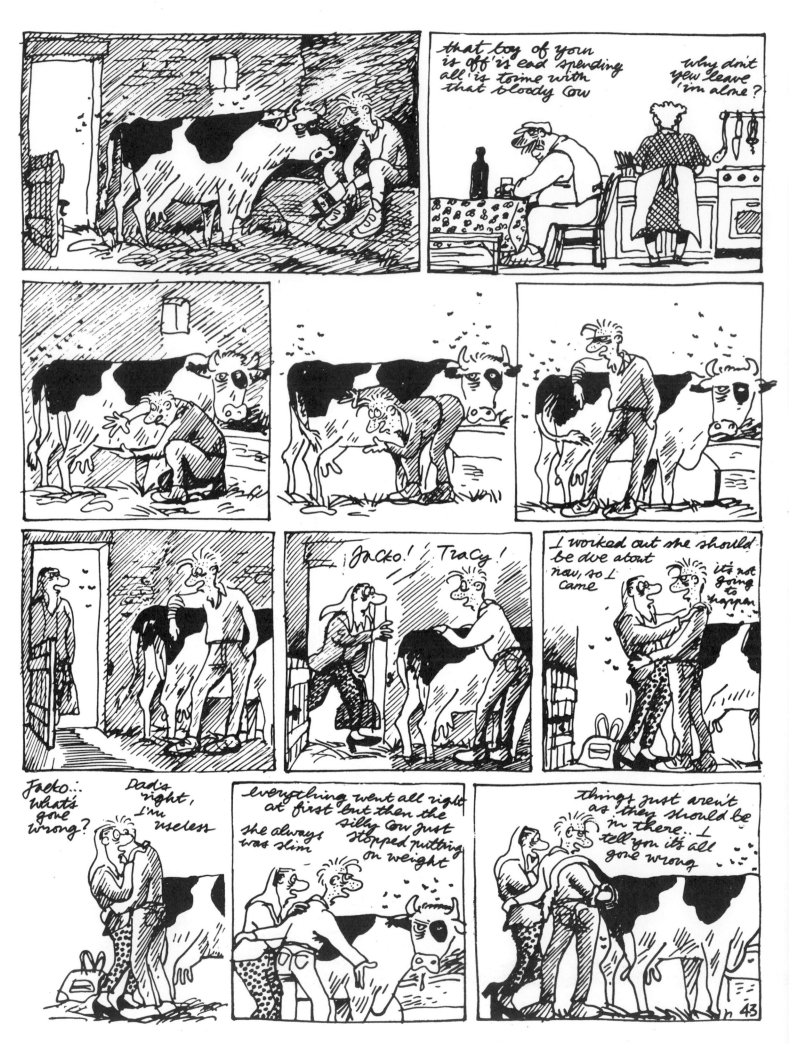

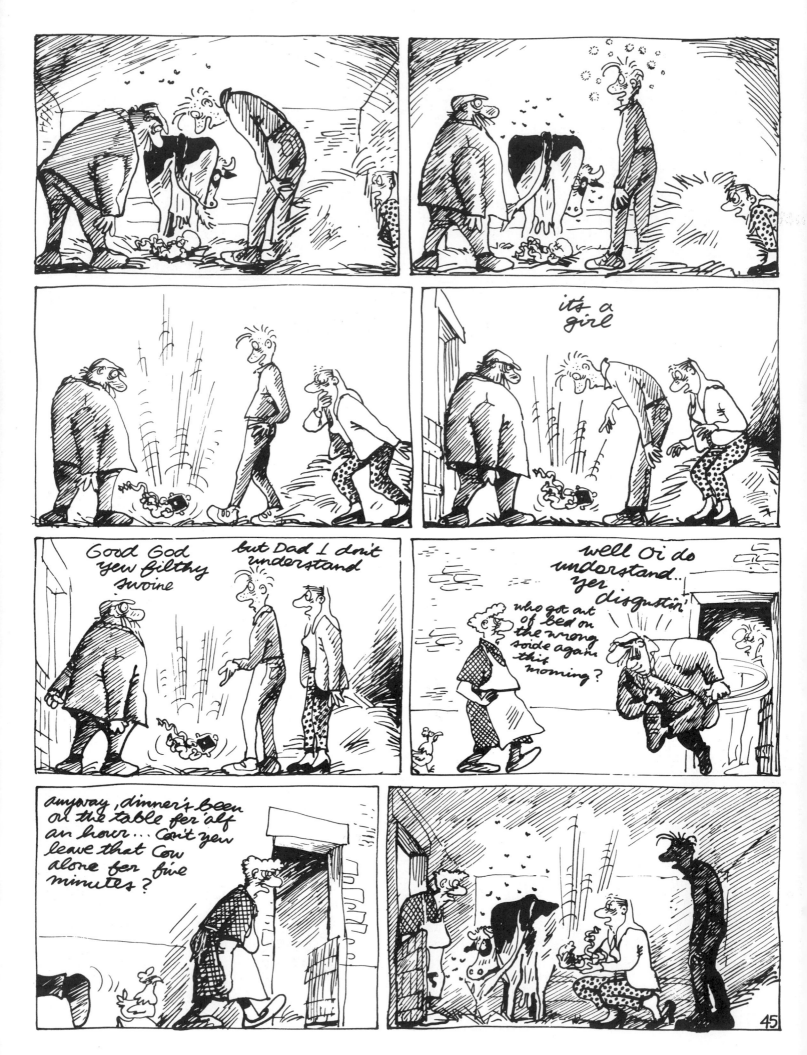

END

Epilogue

RAQUEL SMYTHE'S CAREER TOOK A DECISIVE TURN WHEN SHE MADE "THE FLIGHT OF THE PELICAN" WITH KEN RUSSELL, SCRIPT BY FAY WELDON, AN AUTHOR WE DON'T HEAR SO MUCH ABOUT THESE DAYS.

AFTER THAT SMYTHE MADE ONE FILM AFTER ANOTHER... SHE WAS THE NYMPHET IN "LOLA, LOLA," THE CHILD — BRIDE

IN "I MARRIED A WEREWOLF" AND JESSIE IN "FALL-OUT TWO"

AND OF COURSE THE UNFORGET- TABLE MILDRED, LESBIAN DUCHESS IN "LADIES WHO DO"

SHE ALSO STARRED IN COUNTLESS MINOR PRODUCTIONS

minor productions, listen to him !.. look at the way they've edited that

switch him off Orlando darling, be an angel

CLICK

Orlando darling, all producers and directors are useless

when I think that Roeg gave the role of Zelda to that Richardson girl... but they need a MATUUURE woman for that role... a woman in her sixties; like me

OK so she's pretty, she's got talent ... but at 40 what can she know, what can she feel... it makes me laugh

her voice hasn't started to live... 40 years old... they just let anyone in these days... what can I say?

51

66